NINE YEARS, THREE WEEKS AND THREE DAYS.

A story of Love, Life, Laughter, and Loss.

K.L. Dale

Preface

I didn't know what I was writing when I started. It was just a way for me to get things off my chest, out of my head; losing John affected me in ways I hadn't considered. Writing 'Nine Years' helped me to realise, and appreciate, things I hadn't previously acknowledged as important, or relevant. I never planned on it becoming four parts, it just happened. There were moments when I had to stop writing so I could cry, laugh, think, breathe, let whatever revelation I had had, to sink in. We enjoyed lots of good times over our nine years together, too many to talk about. I have included some of my favourites. We had a good life with lots of laughter, it wasn't all doom and gloom.

I wasn't sure if I would let people read what I was writing at the beginning; it is deeply personal. I've pretty much laid myself, and my life with John, bare for the world to pass judgement on. I haven't sugar coated anything, I have been blunt in some of my wording, that's just the way I am.

This isn't about justifying my grief, I don't need to do that; I refuse to do that. Grief needs no justification.

I would like to think that reading 'Nine Years' will provide an insight into the reality of losing someone you love. To anyone who reads 'Nine Years' who has suffered a loss then I hope you find some kind reassurance that you are not alone in the feelings, thoughts, emotions you have had, or are still experiencing. It is shit, life is very unfair, but we are still standing.

I don't claim to be an expert, I don't have the answers, I do have a story to share.

CONTENTS

Part one

I'd occasionally thought I should write about my experiences. I was never sure when or where to begin? Never sure who would want to read about them, if anyone. Having spent the last couple of hours drinking hot chocolate with a vicar, I thought I'd make a start.

At this moment in time I'm in the throes of the grief cycle. Not a fun place to be. It's not like riding a bike when you're a kid, enjoying the ride. It's not like the fast cycle on your washing machine either, there's no way this is going to last an hour. Fairy non-bio is only slightly cheaper than gin, I don't fancy mixing my non-bio with slim line tonic. So grief in a nutshell; it's shit. There are many ways to describe it, I prefer my way.

I met John in 2009 on one of those classy free online dating websites. Our first date was Wednesday 17th June 2009, we went for a curry and drinks. Nine years, three weeks and three days later I was sat in the hospice, holding John's hand, saying goodbye. Like I just said (and will say several more times); it's shit.

John had first been diagnosed with brain cancer (left frontal lobe Oligodendroglioma to be almost exact) just before his 30th birthday. Four years before we met. John, being the great conversationalist on the subject, didn't talk about it. I just knew that he had had brain surgery to remove a cancerous tumour which as a result he went for quarterly MRI scans. Looking back, I should've known this was an indicator that the cancer could return.

August 2010, barely a year after our first date, John's MRI scan showed the cancer had grown and surgery was necessary, followed by radiotherapy. I went into a spin, for the first of three times. John's response; a holiday in Las Vegas. Less than two weeks after the news we were sitting in the MGM Grand watching a Manchester United game; what else is there to do in Las Vegas? We spent John's birthday at the zoo, it wasn't the greatest zoo in the world, but we had a nice time. On return John had the surgery followed by radiotherapy. John being John just got on with it, his attitude was that he couldn't do anything about it.

The emotions that hit with the word 'cancer' are vast and can be extreme. It's hard to know what to do with these emotions when the person with cancer doesn't communicate. Like I said, John wasn't the best communicator on the subject. I now suspect this was because talking about it would have made it real to him. Dealing with other people and their emotions can be draining. Why put yourself in that position if you don't have to? Why should you have to? I can't imagine the thoughts John may have had. I don't think I want to know.

This is another issue with cancer; it's hard being on the other side. It wasn't me going through it, I did have to watch the effects that the treatments had on John though. It's hard to talk to the untrained person about something so massive. 'People' tried to offer me advice about what I should be doing, how I should be doing it. FYI *never* tell someone they have to be strong for the other person. Who is being strong for the person struggling to cope with the shit situation they find themselves in? Clichés are shit. Nothing did/does wind me up like a 'helpful' cliché: time doesn't heal (it makes it more obvious that something has changed and won't change back), life doesn't go on (it's been fundamentally changed, forever), getting a puppy won't cure all problems, neither would learning to crochet. These are just a small selection of the 'helpful' clichés and pieces of advice I've been

4

offered since John died. On the reverse; people don't know what to say, they feel like they should say something. John would have said; "shut the f**k up" in reply. John could be a man of few words but the ones he used were thoughtful, relevant, knowledgeable, funny, insightful. Some of them were also blunt, direct, potentially offensive. That is what I loved about him.

I miss him.

So now, I'm alone wondering what to do with myself. So far I've redecorated the living room, dining room, hallway, stairs and landing; I say I, I mean the decorator. I've also spent several hours looking at internal oak doors and bathroom suites. Bought and sent back several dresses from various stores. Made a five-hour playlist for my 40th birthday party. Went back to work, albeit unsuccessfully, and volunteered to babysit my niece and nephew. The final pointer is evidence of desperation...they're lovely, really.

The most meaningful thing I've done; made a photobook of John from being a baby to the last ever photo taken of him. There are also photos from his university days (long hair and all); a photo of the medical centre, in Kenya, John helped to build. I included photos of his friends' weddings and associated stag do's; holidays to various places with various friends. John was always up for getting together with his friends, to say he was sociable would be an excellent description. John would be the first one to the bar, more often than not returning with a tray full of Sambuca.

John's last photo, taken on my 39th birthday 2017, is of us in selfie form having enjoyed an evening riverboat cruise in Prague. In hindsight it would've been better to go on the cruise during daylight; due to the darkness of night all we could see was the reflection of us drinking absinthe (we regretted the absinthe the next day), listening to an oompah band on a glass roofed boat surrounded by excitable, aged Italians...guess you had to be there. We had a good night!

My most recent thought project, although I have talked about this for years, is to go tornado chasing. Me, dodging the flying cows of Kansas surrounded by over excitable Americans in a camper van. The latter doesn't appeal but hey ho. When I told John about my tornado chasing idea he stated that I wanted to go and watch people's lives being destroyed by a weather event. I proceeded to bore John with tornado facts and information he really didn't want to know. I couldn't argue with the logic behind John's comment. I on the other hand throw logic to the wind, when it suits me; "F**k it", being a mantra of mine on several occasions.

John was into nature, birds, rivers, lakes, sticklebacks, David Attenborough. I always told him I appreciated nature but ultimately, not my cup of tea. Canada Geese could smell my fear and would taunt me in to shrieking like a tit (not the bird variety) if they came within two metres of me. As an example of our polar opposite personality traits; I love space, stars, meteor showers, full moons, half-moons, planets, constellations. Even though I've seen the ISS fly over dozens and dozens of times I would (and still do) get up, put my coat on and stand like a dedicated nerd, freezing my arse off to watch this ball of light fly over the back garden. John never accepted my invitation to stand outside with me. Saying that; a few years ago during one of the winter meteors showers, John set up two deck chairs in the back garden so we could sit and watch the astrological event, it was freezing cold. We saw a few meteors then scuttled back inside to the warmth. I have wondered how we managed to last nine years...little things like that, and me walking around countless wildlife centres, is how we lasted nine years.

Life before John? I had one. Early life wasn't great: divorce, stepparents, step siblings, school, unfrequented love, spots.... After an unsuccessful spell at Leeds University (too much playing and no studying), and a year in crap jobs, I found myself heading to the Austrian Alps for what turned out to be my first of several chalet seasons. I celebrated my 21st birthday in Saalbach Hinterglem. I was there New Years' Eve 1999. It was an amazing night. I was slightly scared at one point due to the large Austrian bloke next to me waving a red flare around. I'd used hairspray that night, baldness and burns weren't on my agenda. After Austria (summer and winter seasons) I spent two winters in Äkäslompolo in the Finnish Arctic circle (-37 degrees really is cold) followed by the Dolomites of Italy. I spent my final season; summer 2006, working in Morzine, France. Apparently, it was expected I would be home by Christmas; how wrong my doubters were. I have proven the doubters wrong several times since then, I continue to do so to this day.

John had had the Waltons version of an upbringing compared to mine. The home he was brought up in even had a happy name: Gayfields. John was famous for his parties when his parents were away, which was almost every weekend. Obviously I didn't know John then. Hearing him talk about growing up, the parties, his friends (most of whom were still friends with John to the day he died), the holidays, his life in general, was bittersweet. Until his cancer diagnosis John had had a good life. Ignore that, even with his cancer diagnosis, John had a good life. It never stopped him doing anything, it made it more difficult on occasions, but it never stopped him.

There are the holidays we talked about going on. The places we would visit, which zoo we would go to next. There's no reason why I still can't go to these places; a fear of being scared at 35000 feet is a stumbling block, which limits my ability to fly alone. This in turn makes travelling to Kansas, or anywhere that involves leaving the ground on a plane, tricky. Cancer didn't stop John; an irrational fear of flying won't stop me.

By October 2013 we were living together. John had been cancer free (so I thought) for three years, life was pretty good. I'd started my PGCE, John was working full time again and had his driving licence back. Things were fairly non-descript, but in a good way. We went on various holidays (home and abroad), went out for meals, celebrated John's 40th birthday, watched several football matches in the local pub. I suffered The Bored (Lord) of the Rings trilogy several times, the extended Blu-ray editions at four hours plus per film. I did say to John that the worst part of those films was actually the ring bit. It's basically a mythical Brokeback Mountain with two short people, with grossly hairy feet, walking a long way to get rid of a ring, instead of herding cattle in Wyoming. The fighting orcs bit is entertaining. My comments were not appreciated by John, at all.

Jumping forward to August 2016.

After nearly six years John's MRI scan showed the cancer was back. What I found out this time was that the cancer had never gone. There had been a small piece of tumour that hadn't/couldn't be removed. John had known this and never told me. I remember John coming back from the hospital and telling me. Telling me it was inoperable. I cried in the kitchen. I didn't want him to know I was upset - he was the one with cancer and I was crying. Ultimately I couldn't keep it to myself. I hugged him; John wasn't a hugger. He just hugged me back. His 'there's nothing I can do about it' attitude kicked in. That worked for him, it didn't work for me.

The words 'incurable', 'inoperable' were spoken. John was told that chemotherapy was his only option. 'Palliative' was written on his chemotherapy book. It's hard to think back to this time. In real time we had less than two years left together, of course we didn't know that. John never let me go to the hospital with him, not even for scans. This would change. As John's chemotherapy progressed I went to more and more hospital appointments. I met John's MacMillan nurse. John had nine months of chemotherapy. There aren't the words to describe how hard those nine months were. We still managed a trip to Brighton, visiting some of John's old university haunts. May 2017, the outcome was positive. The chemotherapy had shrunk the cancer to its original size, if not smaller. In my mind we were OK. We'd had six years between cancer treatments, there was no reason why this would be any different. We were shown November's MRI scan results. I saw how much brain had been removed through surgery. I saw the speck of cancer in John's frontal lobe. It was good news again; the cancer was stable, see you in four months.

January 14th 2018. I'd been away for the day. I came home to find John sitting on the sofa. He told me his head "felt f**ked", he couldn't describe it. The fact he was telling me was a cause for concern. We went for a walk, a longer walk than I wanted to go on. John collapsed two minutes away from home. That night was the beginning of the end, we just didn't know it.

I'm quite lucky in that the friends I have get my humour. I've enjoyed a three-hour conversation with an old friend who is also unlucky enough to have lost someone to cancer. During our chat she told me her sister, who has terminal cancer, isn't talking to her. I pointed out that she (my friend) will have the last say on the matter. To those of you who gasped in horror: stop reading now. Humour, no matter how macabre, cannot be underestimated.

I'm not sure what I want from writing this. If nothing else I can share my thoughts, even the inappropriate ones. Maybe, you the reader will understand just how hard 2018 has been and why. You'll understand why it isn't improving. John was too young, he was a good bloke, he didn't deserve the death he had.

The same friend told me she had questioned whether she had done enough for her friend. I went above and beyond what I thought I was capable of doing when caring for John. It was both a privilege (that he let me care for him) and a curse. There were times when I wanted to run away, far away from John, from cancer, from my then life. I said several times I wanted my life back. It wasn't till John had gone I realised I wanted the life back I had with John, when John was well. I wanted the times when we went on holiday, made inappropriate jokes about people: John; "he could eat an apple through a letterbox", when referring to an antiques expert's

15

teeth. The mundane life that I hadn't appreciated till it was gone, I wanted it back. I had assumed we had another five years before the cancer would come back. In one way I'm relieved I had this ignorance, on the other hand if I had known I'd have hugged John more...much to his annoyance.

My last five months with John were surreal. Looking back; incredibly stressful. I was suddenly taking care of the man I loved, in a way I had never envisaged.

On the advice of John's MacMillan nurse, I set about making as many new memories as I could in the time we had left. One of my favourites: I drove us to Pooley Bridge in the Lake District, for lunch. We were in the car longer than we were in the cafe eating our sandwiches. The May bank holiday I drove us to the coast for fish and chips. Everywhere was full so we ended up at one of the local pubs, ten minutes away from home. Our last trip out; we sat in the car eating a £3 meal deal watching dog walkers. We were less than five minutes away from home. Jack Johnson's 'Banana Pancakes' was one of the songs we listened to. If I close my eyes and listen to that song I'm back in the car with John. I can picture it like it was an hour ago.

My new role as carer; I was administering anti-sickness tablets followed by chemotherapy medication. I can still tell you all the drugs John was taking, when he had to take them and the dosage. I was on first name terms with his GP, knew all the district nurses, Macmillan staff. I was there for John twenty-four seven. I was there for John before he knew he needed me. John wasn't happy with the visits from his GP, the district nurses, physiotherapists, occupational therapists (to list a few) for the first few months. As he declined he became accustomed to the visitors. John was slowly disappearing before my eyes; not only physically but mentally as well.

Should anyone reading this find themselves in a similar position (I hope you don't); it's shit. Do make the time to tell them you love them, it's too late once they're gone. I told John I loved him more in the last six months of his life than in the previous eight and a half years. I know he felt the same. We developed a closeness that wasn't there before, I can't find the words to describe it. I can tell you I take comfort from knowing we were the strongest we'd ever been over our nine years together; it also makes me miss him more.

11th June 2018, our final trip to the hospital. John's last MRI scan had shown that the chemotherapy hadn't improved the situation. All treatment stopped. It was a case of go home and die. It wasn't said like that. I don't know how I managed to drive us home. I don't know how I held it together as we sat having breakfast in the café. As usual John was calm; or that's how he appeared. I can't remember if I asked him how he felt. I'm sure I would've, I'm sure John would've given me the same stoic answer. We were sat at home that night, John was asleep on the sofa. Looking at him I knew that the hope he had had, had gone. Looking at him I knew we only had weeks left together. Three weeks and one day later John was gone.

I'd been by John's side almost the whole time he was in the hospice. Briefly leaving him for a shower, quick trip to the shop, sleeping in the family room for an hour. One of the doctors we saw told us that sometimes people want to die alone. The story of someone leaving the room for a minute only to return to find their loved one has died. In case this was what John wanted I would tell him when I was going in the shower and give him an estimation of time he had if he wanted to go on his own, he was always there when I got back.

I felt guilty for agreeing to John going into the hospice. Our last real conversation; 25th June, it was clear that John was declining quickly. His speech was going, he knew what he wanted to say, he just couldn't find the words. I knew he understood everything I was saying though. I asked him where he wanted to be at the end. This was the first and only time we discussed him dying. I was crying, John was holding my hand. I once again told him I don't know how he copes. His answer to my question: that no matter where he was it wouldn't be a nice ending. I promised him two things; 1) that he wouldn't be on his own, I would be with him to the end. 2) That he wouldn't know anything about it as I would make sure he was not in pain and well looked after.

28th June, John went into the hospice. I felt so guilty, I was sending him to a hospice. The reality of it was, even with the additional care that was being put in place, I couldn't have coped. That was even more evident during John's last few days, and hours.

That first night in the hospice, John wasn't settled. I knew he wasn't in pain; his eyebrows would've been furrowed if he was. The Midazolam had been given; he was still restless. I spent that first night talking, endlessly to him. I remember talking about 80s films, Tom Hanks in particular. I remember talking about the Back to the Future films, being firm in my opinion that the second film is terrible. I spoke the lyrics to Jack Johnson's song 'Better Together', or the lyrics I could remember.

I have a love hate relationship with Jack Johnson. Back in 2013/14 John was working full time again. With his job came a company car. The car only had a cd player and access to annoying radio stations. Jack Johnson was the only cd in the car. Everywhere we went I had to listen to Jack Johnson. Like all Stockholm Syndrome survivors, I started to like said Mr Johnson. We went through a phase of going to Tesco, very early AM, to do our shopping. Jack Johnson became a part of life.

I don't know at what time John settled; I just know he did. I know the sun was shining outside. In my mind, it was my soothing, dulcet tones that helped John to settle. In reality, it was probably the drugs.

To make John's room less clinical I put up twenty-one photos of him on his wall; various ages, various people in them. All the staff said it was lovely to see John for the person he had been, not who was in the bed.

John had been looking forward to watching the world cup, making light of the reason why he was off work, saying it was the only perk to his situation. We managed to watch a couple of matches together. I say we, John was in the room fast asleep. As it turned out the England matches became bad omens. The first one; John's hospital bed had been delivered; he was now living downstairs in the dining room. That first match John saw 30 minutes in total, if that. The second match John went into the hospice. John died the night of England's success at winning a penalty shoot-out. I lost all interest in the world cup after that. I didn't care who won. John wasn't with me to watch the remaining matches; I wasn't going to bother.

3rd July 2018. The day John died he was totally unresponsive. Previously he would have opened an eye and gave me that smile that showed he knew it was me. The smile that showed me he loved me (in my mind anyway), the smile that showed me John was still there. That had gone. The previous night had been horrendous, I now understand the term 'death rattle'. I kept telling John I loved him. I also told him he could let go whenever he was ready, that I would miss him, but I would be ok. Even though that isn't the case now, I believed it then. It was about 6:30pm, the TV was on, I was sitting next to John reminding him I was still there and that I loved him. John made the strangest gasping sound and he was gone. There was none of this looking peaceful and asleep, John looked dead. The life had gone out of him. One of the nurses had been passing the door just as John gasped, I asked her if she thought John knew I loved him? She simply told me to tell him.

 After John's family had gone it was just me and John in the room. I didn't want to look at him, I didn't want for the last time I looked at him to be his body. Instead, I held his hand. John always had lovely soft, slightly cold hands. I held his hand; it was like he was still with me. I asked him what I was supposed to do without him? How could I survive without him? If he could've answered me I know he would've said something practical, but with a hint of love about it. He would've cuddled me and given me that smile again. Only this time he couldn't.

I've had this theory for years; a beautiful sunrise is when birth, not necessarily physical, occurs. On the reverse a beautiful sunset is when people go to 'heaven' or wherever it is they want to go to. The evening John died the sunset was stunning. Golden with light shining in beams. I knew John was wherever he wanted to be.

I spent that night and few after at my sister's house. I went home the following day to a house full of reminders, John's hospital bed being the biggest. My need to keep busy kicked in. Less than two days after John died; I had registered his death (I made the registrar cry), organised the date, time and place of John's funeral (with his family). John was too young to have a wake, so I organised an after party to celebrate John at the local pub. I went through John's iTunes and made a playlist of songs to be played during the after party. I wrote the toast to be read out when we raised our glasses to John. I did anything and everything to keep busy.

Before I knew it, it was John's funeral. I can't remember if I stayed at home the night before or at my sisters. My best friend was with me by 10am, I think the service was at 2pm. I can't really describe what I was feeling, there were lots of emotions happening at once. I had my first glass of wine long before it would've been socially acceptable (I used my mantra; "F**k it").

Funerals are horrendous. They are a necessary process associated with death. I talked incessantly in the funeral car to the crematorium. It was only when we arrived that reality hit; I was at John's funeral. Mark (the vicar who I drank hot chocolate with) had told me not to hold back, that funerals are the place to be upset, I didn't hold back. I vaguely remember seeing John's coffin and walking in behind it. I heard the Russell Watson song playing (the only thing John ever told me about his funeral was that he wanted this song playing). I took my seat with John's family. I've already said that we met on the romantic platform that is the internet. On top of John's coffin was a picture of him, as suggested by the wonderful Barry (the undertaker) to draw focus away from the coffin. The photo was his profile picture, the first picture I'd ever seen of

John now sat on his coffin. I don't know if that's funny, or not?

There was a friend eulogy, a family eulogy followed by my eulogy. When planning the funeral service with Mark and John's brother, we agreed that there should be a song to break up the service and to give people time to think about John, to reflect on recent events. I chose Jack Johnson's Better Together, there could be no other song.

After that it was prayer time and the funeral was over. As I mentioned, I knew about Russell Watson but that was it. I wanted a song, fitting enough for John, to play as the curtain went around his coffin. AC/DC Back in Black was chosen. The song had been John's ring tone, it was the song he played in pubs and bars whenever he could. I wasn't aware of it, but John friends started nodding when the song started.

I was happy (strange word to use) that so many people attended John's funeral, it proved he was the popular, amazing bloke I thought he was. That was it. Funeral over, now to the after party.

I was beyond drunk. My friend had put a vodka and orange in her bag for me to have straight after the service. I continued to drink the same for the rest of the day. I drank that much vodka and orange the pub ran out of the mixer, no problem, I swapped it to diet coke. The after party is a blur. Mainly due to alcohol consumption and a lack of food. The relief that it was over also played a part.

If a person can have a good funeral, John had a good one. It's shit he had to have one when he did. Forty-three is no age to die. I have often wondered what John would've made of his funeral. Would he have approved? I was told that funerals are for the living. I gave John the funeral that I thought was right; his family agreed.

I think it's only now the enormity of 2018 is hitting. I am angry. Angry John has gone. Angry that I am now alone. Not only am I grieving for John, I'm grieving for the life I'm not going to have with him. Looking back over this year has made me realise how shit it has been. We had thirteen days in 2018 that were good. That weren't dominated by cancer, chemotherapy or hospital appointments. I had thirteen days of being John's partner, instead of carer. How much I've been through and am still going through is becoming apparent. A year ago we were preparing to go to Prague, talking about Christmas presents. I was planning what I was going to cook for our Christmas lunch; I'd promised not to cook nine vegetables like a previous year. I was reminding John he'd need to go in the loft and get the Christmas tree down. Now, I'm alone in the house we shared.

The more 'normal' life becomes the more evident it is that John isn't with me. The space in my life where John was, is getting bigger. I find myself missing him more and more every day. Christmas around the corner isn't helping, it's yet another 'first' to get over. The realisation that I'm not ok was hard enough to face; being not ok and having Christmas at the same time is shit (there's that word again).

There aren't any pearls of wisdom that will make the pain go away. There are of course the clichés that people use when they feel the need to say something, they don't work either. The advice I would offer to someone in my position; I would say that the best thing you can do, is look after you. The world will keep turning, without your input. I'll give this cliché the benefit of the doubt; do take it day by day, hour by hour, whatever pace you need to take, take. If you're not sure then keep things simple. Avoid putting yourself under additional pressure whether at home or work; "f**k it", don't do it. I probably shouldn't be advocating alcohol but, "f**k it", have a large whatever if it will help. Good days will be whatever feels good to you, not someone else's idea. Bad days are shit days, stay in bed if you need to. Watch daytime TV. Homes Under the Hammer is why I pay my TV licence. I will say this though; do not suffer in silence. Seek counselling, GP support, go for a hot chocolate with a friendly vicar, anything that will stop the rot setting in.

I know John didn't want to die but he was never going to get the opportunity to grow old, I have that opportunity, it would be disrespectful to John waste it. I miss John but joining him isn't an option.

So, now what? I don't know. December 2018 I turn forty; I'm not old enough to be forty. It's nineteen years since I feared baldness and burns courtesy of a large Austrian bloke. Ten years since I was crying about turning thirty. My thirties have been a rollercoaster. Highs were high: passing my driving test and graduating from University being amongst my favourites. I don't need to tell you the low points.

Life, so I've been told, begins at forty. I find myself with no ties, I can go anywhere I want (as long as I don't have to fly). When I think about my future with this mind-set I'm almost hopeful. I've proven my doubters wrong in the past, this will be no different. I need to follow my own advice though; not to put myself under pressure to do anything. Kansas isn't going anywhere. I need to think and look before I jump. My "f**k it" mantra is likely to do more harm than good right now. Rushing into another project, or to the extreme, a new life will not ease the pain. It will only delay the inevitable grief process I have to endure.

John will always be a massive part of me. Wherever I go he will be with me.

My eulogy ended with a direct message: "John, I will love and miss you every day." Like death and taxes it's a certainty.

Part two

I feel a bit like Bridget Jones, writing for the world (extreme exaggeration) to read how things are in my life. I never thought I would write a second part; I thought the first part would suffice. Sharing part one with family, and close friends, helped them to understand what this past year has been like for me. It helped them to understand how much it hurts being without John, and why. The longer I am without John the emptier my life feels. I wanted them to understand that what they see, isn't always, what is really going on.

8th December, the day of my 40th birthday party, was as bad as John's funeral. I spent the morning and into early afternoon crying. I didn't know just how guilty I would feel; guilty for wanting to celebrate my birthday without him. I didn't realise just how much I would miss him, want him at my party. I wanted John to come back and tell me it was ok for me to have my party. I wanted to see him again, I wanted him to give me that smile that said so much; of course he didn't, he can't. If I'm honest, if he had appeared before me, I would have had a heart attack.

I seriously considered running away that day. Telling people that the party was off, or that they could party without me. I didn't care, I wanted John, not them. If it wasn't for people travelling from various parts of the country to come to my party, I would've got in my car and driven away. Where would I have gone? The only place I could think of; Pooley Bridge. I was going to go back to the cafe for a prawn sandwich. I would've gone on the steamer boat across Ullswater. I would've sat and watched the world go by. I would've been where the world couldn't find me. I would've been in a place that reminded me of happier times with John. I didn't though; I got the house ready for the people staying over.

Originally, there were five people staying over. Eventually there were just two. I hadn't realised how stressful parties are. The number of people who dropped out in the run up to my party annoyed me. I was on the verge of cancelling it. I didn't.

As it turned out my party was amazing! There must have been nigh on fifty people there. Friends came from all over the country. Even both factions of my family were there. I'd spent the previous couple of weeks learning the dance to Ike and Tina Turner's 'Proud Mary', I shook my arse that night like there was no tomorrow. I loved every minute of my party, the people there made it a great night, the free-flowing gin and tonics will also have helped.

Obviously, John wasn't there; there was a picture of us, taken in Las Vegas, pinned to the marquee curtains. There were also various pictures of me as a child courtesy of my dad and sister. My sister had also included photos from my chalet days, of us dressed up as Princess Leia (me) and the worlds shortest Darth Vader (her). There was a good selection of photos that covered my forty years. My actual birthday was uneventful, pleasant enough, but uneventful. It involved onion bhajis, lamb rogan josh and prosecco...classy.

It's six months since John died. I had no understanding or appreciation back then of how draining grief is, mentally and physically. I assumed grief was sadness and crying, there is a lot of that. Fundamentally it's all consuming, there is no way to control it. I still find myself wanting to text John when I've had a good day, bad day, have seen something funny, have gossip (that he would have no interest in). John was always the first person I'd text, or call. I would text John when I'd been to the hairdressers, just so he would remember to notice.

People ask me how I'm doing, how's work (no idea since I'm not there), they tentatively ask me about my plans for Christmas (I'm staying with my sister). I ask the polite questions that are expected at this time of year; I can't say I'm always interested in the answers.

I saw my counsellor this week. I don't know what I would do without Liz, she gets it, she gets me. You could argue that it's her job, it is, but it doesn't feel like that. I told Liz that if I'd been in John's shoes (all size 13 of them) I'd have been off, travelled the random David Attenborough places of the world. What I realised during our conversation; John normalised his life. Doing extraordinary things would have highlighted the one thing John didn't want to acknowledge as having a power over him.

I would like to know what John would make of my writing. I would be very surprised if he read them. John would want a synopsis, the abridged version, the key points in bullet form...unlike his Bored of the Rings extended Blu-ray collection.

One thing I'm very aware of at the minute; there are a limited number of days left that I can say something positive about a year ago. This time last year we'd be going to Tesco for our Christmas food shopping, John would be spending hours perfectly wrapping presents. We'd be using the Christmas plates, listening to the age-old Christmas songs. We'd be cancer free. I have until January 13th 2019 to look back to happy memories, after that it's all downhill. It's all cancer, cancer, cancer.

It just adds to the feeling of being consumed by grief. It's like I said last time; bad days are shit days. I've been without John for six months and I want him back; that's not going to happen, I know that, I know I have to carry on...I just don't always want to. That's not say you need to give me the crisis team number, I just mean some days it's just me, Martin, Dion and Lucy/Martel (Homes Under the Hammer presenters for those who work for a living) and that's all I can manage. I have accepted that John has gone, I don't like it, but I don't have a choice.

John isn't coming back. Life can be ridiculously unfair.

It's now 'secondary' grief I'm having to deal with. All the random things that John would've (eventually) done, I now have to. I don't know the first thing about owning a house, electrics, plumbing, gardening. I'm having to learn about it, and I hate it. If John was still here with me, it would be up to him sort the dodgy electrics. Every decision I make without John makes me miss him more. It's these 'secondary' bits that are making the black hole of grief even harder to avoid. Don't get me wrong, I will do my utmost to avoid said hole, but, I know Martin and co are waiting for me on the days I can't be arsed to fight.

It's head versus heart time. I know what I should do: go back to work, get back to "normal" life. I don't know if I can. I used to love my job; I'm worried I don't anymore. My outlook on life has changed, my attitude has changed. Do I have the capacity to give a shit? What do I do if I don't? I mentioned in my last writing that I have proven my doubters wrong in the past. Maybe, at this moment in time I am my biggest doubter?

Something else I've realised, thanks to Liz; people do think they know what the dead person would say in a situation: "John would want you to enjoy yourself", John would want this, John would want that. I'm tempted to directly quote John again. John rarely gave his opinion unless I asked for it. He would give me a rare hug, let me rant, cry, talk...but he *never* told me what I should do. Ultimately John knew I would do the best thing for the situation, for me, for us. I knew he had my back; I wish he still did.

Writing this is making me realise just how much we loved each other. John wasn't a great romantic but when he tried, he did it right. During our nine years together John bought me flowers three times: our first date he rocked up with two dozen red roses, I didn't own a vase. The second time was my birthday, probably my 31st, they were stunning. The last time was the day before he started radiotherapy, a large bunch of purple tulips. I can't look at purple tulips the same way.

That's not to say John didn't do romance at other times: we went to the park for a picnic...red wine, fresh bread, a blanket to sit on. It was the perfect way to spend an afternoon. The day I passed my driving test. John took me out to celebrate, he hijacked the music system in the bar to play my driving song (Imagine Dragons, It's Time). Something else I talked about in my eulogy; I made a list of all the things we did together over the nine years, it's a long list of various outings, holidays, weekends away, day trips, meals out, nights in, visits to various pubs, concerts, comedy clubs, visiting friends and family. We had a good life together, a funny life, it was too short, but good, nonetheless.

There is the potential for whatever this is to become negative, focused on the dark side of life. At this moment in time it is hard to see brighter days on the horizon. I've talked about the last year, in reality it was a never-ending roller coaster of a life with John. Every three months John would go for an MRI scan, every three months we would wait for the result. I will admit that I had become complacent prior to August 2016. In my mind the cancer had been removed by the surgery in 2010, the radiotherapy had blasted whatever bits had been left. We were in the clear, on the path to growing old together. August 2016 changed that.

August 2016. I was teaching adults: employability skills, along with a variety of other courses. April 2017, I took some time off; I had more important things to think about. John's chemotherapy was coming to an end; the side effects caused by the accumulation of eight months of treatment were evident. I wanted to spend my time with John, we didn't know the outcome of the chemotherapy at that time. I was preparing myself for the worst but hoping for the best.

John never lost his hair; it wasn't a side effect of his chemotherapy. I wasn't aware of how many different types of chemotherapy exist until that time. It's not a one treatment fits all cancers. 2016-17. I wasn't involved with John's chemotherapy the first time around. It was split between IV and tablets. John was in control; he knew what he was doing.

What I didn't depress you with in the first part was that the cancer had spread from John's frontal lobe, to his temporal lobe. There was no sign of it in November, we both saw the MRI scan. John's neurosurgeon knows his stuff; he wouldn't have missed it. The cancer in John's temporal lobe was bright white and the size of a thumb print. Something else I've learnt through my own research (don't quote me, I'm not a doctor or an expert);

malignant tumours appear brighter on scans; John's temporal lobe was lit up like Christmas. Macabre humour.

The night John collapsed he lost comprehension, he couldn't get his words out in any order, how much he actually understood was questionable. The temporal lobe controls speech and understanding...amongst other things. I managed to understand what he was saying though. John's speech returned, although not exactly to what it had been prior to his collapse. What followed in the few weeks between John collapsing and seeing the MRI scan results was pure shitness; that's not a real word, it should be. After the scan result, with the neurosurgeon, came the wait to see the oncologist and to start chemotherapy. I had a sinking feeling, I knew the next few months would be hard, I didn't expect the eventual outcome.

I was talking to John's Macmillan nurse on a regular basis, there was nothing I could ask that she wouldn't or couldn't answer. John was given a different chemotherapy treatment, tablet form only, no IV. Medication to be taken at home, providing blood tests were ok.

I don't know what happened, John appeared to understand the instructions; take all six chemotherapy tablets at once, one hour after the anti-sickness medication. Something went wrong. John took the first dosage wrong; I didn't realise till it was too late. Why would I check John was taking his chemotherapy correctly when he previously had? After that I took control of his chemotherapy. I took control of all his medications, it wasn't worth the risk of him taking them wrong again, it was too important. John didn't argue against it.

2018. Things had massively improved on my job front at this point; I'd left my previous employer. I now had (still have) a job I loved (I hope I still do). There was no question in my mind though; John came before everything and everyone else. I didn't want to have any regrets about leaving him with others while I went to work, I wasn't doing that again. We would go out for breakfast, meeting family or friends. Morning was the best time of the day to do anything, John was exhausted without doing a great deal. It wasn't just the chemotherapy that was affecting John, but the cancer itself. I put my life on hold for John. I assumed, wrongly as it turned out, that I would be able to pick up my life where I left it. I can't, that life no longer exists.

It wasn't the total doom and gloom I've portrayed so far; it was shit (there's that word, again) but we also laughed, made the most of the times John felt up for going out. John's dry sense of humour hadn't diminished; he could still cut a person in half with his dry, caustic wit: Three weeks after passing my driving test I drove us down to Kent, bitching A1 and the M25 on the way, I was chuffed to bits! John congratulated me for driving down long, straight roads. That might sound harsh out of context,

John's humour made me love him more. I thought I had a dry sense of humour; then I met John.

I remember one day he thanked me for looking after him, I didn't really know what to say, I wish I'd just told him he was welcome. I wish I'd taken the opportunity to hug him.

Next week is Christmas. I was guaranteed two presents off John: a box of Lindor white chocolate truffles (aka white balls of pleasure) and a diary. Christmas 2014; I adopted a sloth, from Chester Zoo, for John. Why a sloth? Purely based upon John's activity levels. My niece once told me she didn't know John was 6'7", he was always sitting down when she saw him...out of the mouths of babes. Included in the adoption pack: a picture of said sloth, an adoption certificate and two admissions tickets. John's name was added to the plaque in the sloth enclosure, along with many others who adopted a sloth that year. That was probably the best present I ever bought John; he was hard to buy presents for. If John wanted something he went out and bought it. Whatever it was it had to be the newest, most up to date, the biggest...John bought 'us' a 55" smart TV. John was also generous, especially when it came to Sambuca....and cars! When I passed my driving test John part exchanged his beloved Saab for my Ford KA, if that isn't love then what is?! We went to Chester for a midweek break so we could go and see John's sloth. We stayed in the hotel next to the racecourse, we had a lovely few days away. Out of the zoos we went to, Chester was our favourite.

The first six months of my 2018 diary was all John orientated: hospital appointments, MRI scans, blood tests, chemotherapy, GP visits, district nurse visits, new medications. I also wrote in the times we went out for breakfast, lunch, coffee and cake.

I became a voice for the dairy intolerant. John couldn't eat dairy, everywhere we went I would be asking what dairy free cakes or biscuits were available: gluten free; you're laughing, you're well catered for. Dairy free; you're going hungry or farting like a trooper for dallying in the forbidden land of dairy.

We went away for Easter to the Lake District. We made the usual visit to Pooley Bridge. I can't say that was a particularly restful break. John was becoming more and more breathless with the shortest of walks. I phoned his Macmillan nurse, spoke to his GP. I did consider changing my GP to John's but decided against it, stalking charges didn't appeal. Over the course of the conversations it was decided that it would be a good idea for John to go to hospital; a side effect of John's chemotherapy: blood clots on the lungs. I told John this; he wasn't going to hospital. I told him that blood clots are life threatening; he wasn't going to hospital; I was blunt and told him he could die; he wasn't going to hospital. I gave up, I wasn't going to force the issue. John had made his mind up; he wasn't going anywhere near a hospital. The term 'capacity' started to be spoken more and more. John understood the risk he was taking. We spent the remaining couple of nights in the Lake District, not going far or doing much. The view from our room was stunning.

This may, or may not, shock you. I already knew at that point John wouldn't survive, it was when he would die, not if. If John was going to die due to a blood clot, then it didn't really matter where he was, he loved the Lake District, let him die there. I wasn't playing God; I was doing what John wanted. As soon as we got home though, I took him to the hospital. John wasn't happy. I'd followed his wishes in the Lakes, it was his turn. As it turned out John didn't have a blood clot. We were simply told, by a twelve-year old looking doctor, it was cancer related; no shit, Sherlock. John would have been seriously annoyed (putting it mildly) with me if I'd made him go to hospital in the Lakes. We never went away again after that. Short trips only: the high street cafe for breakfast; the local pub for lunch; to known dairy free, friendly coffee shops; the local park...anywhere with close proximity to home, or the hospital.

The blood clot story is one of the many examples where I put John's wishes before my own. The stress of those few days in the Lakes was almost unmanageable. I survived by knowing that I was doing what John wanted. I was still, *very*, annoyed with him.

In my next life; I want to be a goddess, worshipped for being wonderful. Given I don't buy into religion it's unlikely to happen, my agnostic little toe won't save me. Will there be another part? I don't know, I suspect there will be. If nothing else I have Christmas to survive followed quickly by new year. I've never been a big fan of new year; John could take or leave it as well. I suspect, if John was here, we would have ended up ordering a Chinese take away and watching Bored of the Rings. I still might. I'm not going to tempt fate. I sincerely hope I don't, ever, have another year like this one. That cliché about what doesn't kill you makes you stronger, like the majority of them, is rubbish. The only reason I have survived, so far, is down to family (John's, not just my own), friends, a friendly vicar, counselling, Mirtazapine, crying, laughing, the discovery of pink gin and, of course, Homes Under the Hammer.

I can't say life was always easy with John, it wasn't. Would I do it all again, knowing what was coming? Yes. Why, you might ask? John, like L'Oréal, is worth it.

Part three

The build up to Christmas wasn't great, to say the least. I thought about John, a lot. I was trying to remember our last Christmas together. I can't remember what I bought John for Christmas. I can't remember if I cooked turkey or beef for lunch. None of that matters, I know we enjoyed our usual chilled out day.

Driving to my sister's I realised that I have to make the best of a sad situation, I don't have a choice. As I pulled out of the driveway I looked back at the house. If John was still here, we'd be in the pub by now, a Christmas eve tradition that pre-dates my existence in John's life. I'd be on my second gin and tonic; pints of lager seem old hat now. We'd be sat where John's picture hangs, in the back room of the pub. Christmas eve; I'd prepare enough food to feed the street; or in a previous life, a chalet full of hungry skiers in the Austrian alps. I usually opened most of my presents when we got home from the pub; it was Christmas day. Christmas day, neither of us would be feeling lively. It didn't matter, it was just us in our own world. Cooking Christmas dinner in my scotty dog pyjamas was liberating. Out of our nine Christmases together we spent six of them on our own; they were the best Christmases.

I did think about adopting a sloth again this year, John's name back up on Chester Zoo's sloth enclosure wall. I haven't, it wouldn't serve a purpose.

I'm sat looking at pictures of us; I'd love to travel back in time. I want to enjoy those moments again. I would make the most of them, make the hug last a few seconds longer, spend an extra second looking at his face. Listen more intently to whatever John was saying. I miss his voice. John's wearing the same suit, shirt and tie in both pictures. I'm putting together a memory box of John; I've included that tie.

Sitting, thinking about John, thinking about life, I have this image in my head of a long dark road ahead. Nothing is making me excited for the future. I just see a life without John, a life I don't want. There are moments when a sense of clarity hits, it's a relief. The black moments turn grey and kind of light appears. Daring to think about the future is scary, I'm not leaving John behind, I'm doing what John would want me to and I have to remember that. John was a huge part of my life for nine years. The way I lost him was traumatic, horrific, heart-breaking, the list of adjectives I could use is almost endless.

If I'm honest with myself I always knew I would end up on my own, John was never going to win his 'fight' against cancer. I hate that phrase 'fight against cancer'; cancer is a process, there are steps that happen regardless of the type of cancer a person has: diagnosis, treatment, outcome. That is a simplified version, you may have your own thoughts. That's the process I witnessed with John, unfortunately John didn't get a positive outcome. Saying that, John had fourteen years from diagnosis to the day he died, not everyone gets that.

Just as cancer has a process, so does grief. Death is final, the end of the road, game over. Grief is the exact opposite: never ending, ongoing, draining. I do wonder, if things had been different and it was me that died, would John be ok? I think so. I would be very surprised if he redecorated the house or watched as much Homes Under the Hammer as I have.

I wish I had the key to make grief easy, I wish such a key existed. It doesn't. Time doesn't heal, it highlights what we have lost. Time is needed in order to adjust to life without the person you love, in my case John. 'Adjusting' doesn't mean you miss them any less, it doesn't mean all is happy in the garden again. I love John just as much today as I did six days, six months, six years ago. I miss him more today than I did yesterday.

I've previously told you that the night John died the sunset was stunning. I have images in my head of 'heavenly' John sat in the pub watching the football; sat at home playing on his play station; sat on the blue leather monstrosity of a sofa watching the mythical Brokeback Mountain trilogy. Wherever John is, he is ok.

I think if there is a fight associated with cancer, it's the families who fight every day. Everyday life still goes on; the world doesn't stop when cancer appears. John had cancer, everyone who loved him was helpless (as was John, he certainly didn't choose to have cancer) we couldn't do anything, apart from make life comfortable and as normal as possible. That's a hard fight.

John was very much a closed book, if your question wasn't worded in a succinct, specific manner you weren't getting the answer you were hoping for. Not talking about it, putting it to one side, could have been John's way of ignoring the inevitable. Not facing up to something means it's not real, not happening. I could be wrong; it wouldn't be the first time. I was talking to one of John's friends at my party, talking about how if anyone did ask John how he was, they would get a selection of one-word answers: "fine", "good", "alright", "ok", being common responses. Not many people, successfully, pressed John for more information.

John was never rude when his friends asked him questions, he knew they were asking out of concern. Ultimately if he didn't want to answer the question, you knew it.

Part four

It's the middle of January 2019, two weeks since my last writing. It feels like I'm entering the calm after the storm. Looking back, December was horrific; three big events, all without John. I survived though, mentally battered and bruised, but here I am.

I've been looking back over my previous writings. The feelings I talked about are as raw, and relevant, now as they were then. I now have to say John died last year, that makes it sound much longer than it actually is. I almost feel like I should be 'cured', no longer riding the grief cycle. I know that's rubbish. I do feel like I've moved into a different place, possibly because life feels calmer right now, the big hurdles I was dreading have been and gone. Who knows how long this calm will last? Am I more prepared for future hurdles? I doubt it.

I am aware I'm starting to jump from one project to another again, the need to keep busy is still there. Will I burn out? Will I pass go and collect £200? Who knows?

My big plans: dodging flying cows in Kansas; I've seen the Northern Lights, I'd like to see the Southern Lights as well; are going to continue to take a back seat, for now. It would be nice to go back to Austria one day, enjoy kaiserschmarrn and a cheeky flugerl, again there's no urgency to plan anything. I've already decided I want to be away for John's anniversary, I was there the first time.

Life is too short; I know that. That fateful bus might get me tomorrow, so be it. I don't want to, or need to, push myself into situations that I don't feel ready for. I'm going to enjoy what is on my doorstep; I'm two hours away from the Lake District, half an hour away from the coast, there's nothing stopping me jumping in the car and driving off. The world is a big place, exploring starts with small steps.

I, and maybe you, can see how my grief, thoughts and feelings have evolved. They are also circling back over. I started writing in late October/early November 2018, that's only three months ago, it feels much longer. The rollercoaster of emotions I've shared with you have been draining, but also inevitable. I have no choice but to ride the rollercoaster, I can't get off; you however could stop reading at any time, close the cover and go back to your everyday life…I'm jealous.

It feels like I've come to a natural conclusion, for now. I don't need to reiterate what I've said; you all know I love and miss John. Will there be part five? I don't know. Who knows what life has in store for me next?

I feel like I should end with a profound thought, a piece of wisdom that you the reader can take away that makes you feel warm and fuzzy; I don't have one. I can make a suggestion though; put Homes Under the Hammer on, Martin and co might be just what you need.

Please take a minute to leave a review on Amazon or Goodreads!

Follow *@kathNineYears* on Twitter

Nine Years, Three Weeks and Three Days on Facebook

<u>OUT NOW</u>

Time Flies By Slowly.

A story of Love, Life, Laughter, and Loss Continued.

DISCLAIMER

Some names and identifying details have been emitted to protect the privacy of individuals. All thoughts and opinions within 'Nine Years' are my own; no offence is intended or meant to influence the reader.

Printed in Great Britain
by Amazon

57681496R00041